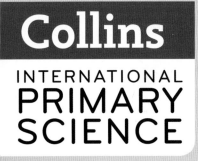

Collins

INTERNATIONAL PRIMARY SCIENCE

Student's Book 1

T0340553

William Collins' dream of knowledge for all began with the publication of his first book in 1819. A self-educated mill worker, he not only enriched millions of lives, but also founded a flourishing publishing house. Today, staying true to this spirit, Collins books are packed with inspiration, innovation and practical expertise. They place you at the centre of a world of possibility and give you exactly what you need to explore it.

Collins. Freedom to teach.

Published by Collins
An imprint of HarperCollins*Publishers* Ltd.
The News Building
1 London Bridge Street
London
SE1 9GF

HarperCollins*Publishers*
Macken House,
39/40 Mayor Street Upper,
Dublin 1,
D01 C9W8, Ireland

Browse the complete Collins catalogue at
www.collins.co.uk

MIX
Paper | Supporting responsible forestry
FSC™ C007454

This book contains FSC™ certified paper and other controlled sources to ensure responsible forest management.

For more information visit: www.harpercollins.co.uk/green

© HarperCollins*Publishers* Limited 2021

10 9 8 7 6

ISBN: 978-0-00-834090-2

Second edition

Contributing authors: Phillipa Skillicorn, Karen Morrison, Tracey Baxter, Sunetra Berry, Pat Dower, Helen Harden, Pauline Hannigan, Anita Loughrey, Emily Miller, Jonathan Miller, Anne Pilling, Pete Robinson.

All rights reserved. No part of this publication may be reproduced, stored in a retrieval system, or transmitted in any form by any means, electronic, mechanical, photocopying, recording or otherwise, without the prior written permission of the Publisher or a licence permitting restricted copying in the United Kingdom issued by the Copyright Licensing Agency Ltd, 5th Floor, Shackleton House, 4 Battle Bridge Lane, London SE1 2HX.

British Library Cataloguing in Publication Data
A Catalogue record for this publication is available from the British Library.

Commissioning editor: Joanna Ramsay
Product manager: Letitia Luff
Development editor: Karen Williams
Project manager: 2Hoots Publishing Services Ltd
Proofreader: Caroline Low
Cover designer: Gordon MacGilp
Cover illustrator: Ann Paganuzzi
Image researcher: Emily Hooton
Illustrators: Beehive Illustration (John Batten, Moreno Chiacchiera, Phil Garner, Kevin Hopgood, Tamara Joubert, Simon Rumble, Jorge Santillan)
Internal design and typesetting: Ken Vail Graphic Design Ltd
Production controller: Lyndsey Rogers
Printed and bound in India by Replika Press Pvt. Ltd.

With thanks to the following teachers and schools for reviewing materials in development: Preeti Roychoudhury, Sharmila Majumdar and Sujata Ahuja, Calcutta International School; Hawar International School; Melissa Brobst, International School Budapest; Rafaella Alexandrou, Diana Dajani, Sophia Ashiotou and Adrienne Enotiadou, Pascal Primary School Lefkosia; Niki Tzorzis, Pascal Primary School Lemesos; Vijayalakshmi Chillarige, Manthan International School; Taman Rama Intercultural School.

Registered Cambridge International Schools benefit from high-quality programmes, assessments and a wide range of support so that teachers can effectively deliver Cambridge Primary.

Visit www.cambridgeinternational.org/primary to find out more.

Contents

Topic 1 Plants

In this topic you will learn that plants and animals are living things. You will also learn that there are living things and things that have never been alive. Lastly, you will learn the main parts of a flowering plant and about the things that plants need to survive.

1.1 **All about Science**

Key words
• investigation
• prediction

Science is about exploring the world around us. To learn about the world, you need to ask questions and then choose how to find the answers. You can use science words to talk about how and why things happen.

1 Look at the pictures. Describe the different plants you can see. ▶ ▼

2 What is the boy doing? Why do you think the boy is doing this?

Investigations can help you find answers to questions and to understand the world better. Before you do an investigation, it can be useful to say what you think will happen. This is called making a **prediction**. You can use observations and things you already know to help you make a prediction. Remember to describe your prediction well.

1 Look at the pictures on page 1 of your Workbook. Predict what you think will happen next. Why do you think this?

2 A boy has two plants. The boy waters one plant every day. The boy forgets to water the other plant. Will the plants look the same? Describe what you think the plants will look like.

3 Look at the picture. What question do you think the children asked?

4 How can the children find the answer to their question?

5 What do you predict will happen to the plants? Explain your prediction using 'I think…because…'

Making predictions is an important skill. A good prediction shows that you understand science well.

I have learned

- I can ask and answer questions to learn about the world.

- Investigations can help me to find answers to questions.

- Things that I can see and things that I know can help me to make a good prediction.

3 Do an investigation to find out what happens to plants that do not get water. Make predictions and record your observations on page 2 of your Workbook. Were your predictions correct?

1.2 Is it alive?

Everything in the world around us is either **living** or **non-living**.

1 What can you see in the picture? ▼

2 Which things are living?

3 Which things are non-living?

4 Which of these things are living? ▼

5 Which are non-living?

1 Make a poster to show living and non-living things.

2 Go on a walk around your school. Make two lists to show how many living and how many non-living things you can see.

3 Name some living and some non-living things. Choose one living thing and describe it to your partner.

I have learned

- Everything is either living or non-living.

1.3 Plants and animals are living things

Key words
- plant
- animal
- alive

There are many different types of living things. We can sort all living things into groups. The two main groups are **plants** and **animals**. If something is **alive**, it is a plant or an animal.

1 Which things in the picture are living?

6

2 Which things in the picture are non-living?

3 Sort the living things into plants and animals.

4 Count how many different types of plants you can see.

5 Say how the plants are different from each other.
Say how they are the same.

Activities

1 Name some living things and ask your partner to say if they are plants or animals.

2 Look at the list of living things that you found around your school last lesson. Label each thing *plant* or *animal*. Can you name some of the plants and animals?

3 Draw or write about one plant and one animal that you know. Describe each one. Say how they are the same and how they are different.

I have learned

- Plants and animals are living things.
- If something is alive, it is a plant or an animal.

1.4 Things that have never been alive

Key words
- non-living
- alive
- living

Some **non-living** things were once **alive**.
These things come from plants and animals.

Wood comes from trees. We use wood for many things.
Trees are **living** but wood is non-living. When wood is cut
from a tree it stops growing, so the wood is no longer alive.

Some things have never been alive, such as water, stone,
metal and plastic.

1. How many non-living things can you find in the picture?

2. Which non-living things were once alive?

3. Which non-living things have never been alive?

4. What does a tree do that a table made from wood does not do?

Activities

1 Look at the pictures on page 5 of your Workbook. Circle the things that have never been alive.

2 Walk around your classroom. Find some non-living things that were once alive and some things that have never been alive. Make a list.

3 Make an odd-one-out poster of things that were once alive and things that have never been alive.
Can your classmates guess the odd one out?

I have learned

- Some non-living things were once alive.

- Some things have never been alive.

1.5 Parts of a plant

Plants come in many different shapes, sizes and colours. Plants can look very different but they all have **roots**, **stems** and **leaves**. Some plants also have **flowers**.

1 Compare the plants in the pictures. ▼
Describe how they are the same.
Describe how they are different.

A

flower

stem

B

leaves

roots

2 Do both plants have leaves?

3 Do both plants have flowers?

Different plants have different types of roots. We can eat some roots such as carrots.

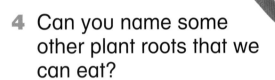

4 Can you name some other plant roots that we can eat?

5 We can eat other parts of some plants. Can you name two?

Activities

1 Compare two local plants. Draw or write about the differences on page 7 of your Workbook.

2 Draw and label a flowering plant on page 8 of your Workbook.

3 Go outside and look at a tree. Draw and label a picture of the tree and make a leaf rubbing.

I have learned

- All plants have some parts that are the same.
- Some plants have flowers.
- We can eat some parts of some plants.

1.6 What do plants need to survive?

Key words
- water
- light
- grow
- soil
- air
- healthy

Whichever environment a plant lives in, it needs **water** and **light** to live and **grow** well.

Without enough water and light, a plant will die.

Most plants also need **soil, air** and warmth to be **healthy**.

A

B

C

1 Look at the pictures. ▲ ▶
What things are the
same about the plants?
What things are different?

2 What do you think
has happened to the
unhealthy plants?

3 Why is a hot desert not a good environment for most plants?

Activities

1 Make a poster to show the things plants need to live and grow well.

2 In what way do you think light affects the growth of plants? Predict what you think will have happened to a plant that has been kept in the dark. Draw a picture on page 9 of your Workbook.

3 Examine two plants. One has been in the light and the other has been in the dark. What has happened? Why? Record your observations on page 10 of your Workbook. Was your prediction correct?

I have learned

- Plants need light and water to grow well.
- Plants also need soil, air and warmth to be healthy.
- If a plant does not get enough light or water, it will die.

Looking back **Topic 1**

In this topic you have learned

- Plants and animals are living things.
- Living things are the same in some ways and different in some ways.
- Some non-living things were once alive. Some things have never been alive.
- All plants have roots, stems and leaves. Some plants have flowers.
- Plants need light and water to grow well. They also need soil, air and warmth to be healthy.

How well do you remember?

1 Which of these non-living things was once alive? Which thing has never been alive?

2 Make a list of the different types of plants you can see near your school.

3 Look at these plants. Say how they are the same. Say how they are different.

4 Draw and label your favourite plant on page 12 of your Workbook. What does your plant need to survive?

Topic 2 Humans and other animals

In this topic you will learn the main parts of the human body. You will explore the senses and find out which part of the body each sense uses. You will also learn what animals need to survive. Lastly, you will learn that all humans have things that are similar and things that are different.

15

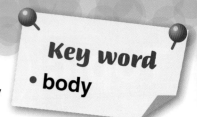

Key word
• body

2.1 **Parts of the human body**

Humans may look different but they all have the same parts of the **body**. The body parts have different names.

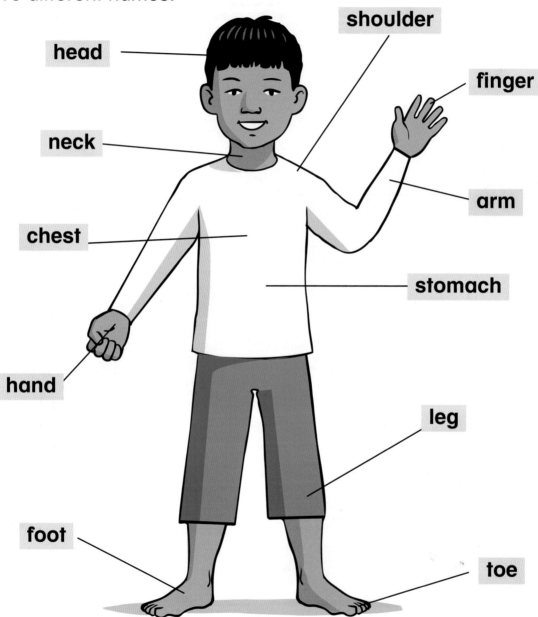

shoulder

head

finger

neck

arm

chest

stomach

hand

leg

foot

toe

1 Look at the picture. ▲
How many parts of the body do you know?

2 Point to each body part on your own body.

3 Look at the picture. ▲
How many different parts of the body can you see?

4 What are the girls doing with their hands?

Activities

1 Name some different clothes. Match each one to the correct body part.

2 Talk about the different parts of your body that you use when you are playing games with your friends.

3 Draw and label a picture of yourself on page 13 of your Workbook.

I have learned

- Humans have the same body parts.
- The body parts have different names.

2.2 Our senses

Key words
• sense organ
• senses

Humans have five **sense organs**.
We use each sense organ for a different **sense**.

We use our **eyes** to see. This is our sense of **sight**.

We use our **ears** to hear. This is our sense of **hearing**.

We use our **nose** to smell. This is our sense of **smell**.

We use our **tongue** to taste. This is our sense of **taste**.

We use our **skin** to feel. This is our sense of **touch**.
Our bodies are covered in skin.

1 What is the girl doing? Which sense organs is the girl using?

2 What are the boys doing? Which sense are they using?

Other animals also have senses which tell them about their environment. Senses help animals to find food and to stay safe.

Many animals have very good senses of sight, hearing and smell.

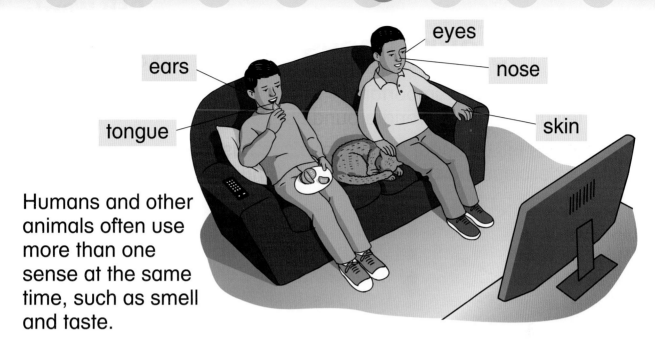

eyes

ears

nose

tongue

skin

Humans and other animals often use more than one sense at the same time, such as smell and taste.

3 Look at the picture. ▲ Which senses are the children using?

4 Which sense organs do you use when you eat an orange?

5 What happens to your sense of taste when you have a cold?

Activities

1 Match each sense with its sense organ on page 14 of your Workbook.

2 Think about eating a meal with your family. Which senses do you use? Why?

3 Label the picture on page 15 of your Workbook and complete the sentences to say what each sense can do.

I have learned

- Humans have five sense organs and five senses.
- We often use more than one sense at a time.

2.3 Using our senses

Our **senses** are very important.
They tell us about the world around us.

Our senses tell us about good things such as the taste of delicious food and the sound of music.

1 Which sense organs are the family in the picture using? ▲

2 What can the family's senses tell them about different things on the beach?

Our senses also warn us about bad things, such as the smell of fire or the taste of sour milk.

Our senses can warn us about **danger** and help keep us **safe**.

3 What can the people in the picture hear? ▲
What can they see?

4 Describe how your senses help to keep you safe when you cross a busy road.

5 Can you use more than one sense at the same time?

Activities

1 Listen to some sounds. Write down what you hear on page 16 of your Workbook.

2 Choose one sense and make a poster to show how that sense can help you in daily life.

3 Go on a sensory hunt. Make a list of everything you observe with your senses. Choose one place and draw what you observed there. Which sense did you use the most?

I have learned

- Our senses tell us about our environment.
- Our senses help us to stay safe.

Key word
• sense organ

2.4 **Users of science**

Our senses tell us about the environment around us. Senses help us to survive and stay safe.

It is important that we look after our **sense organs** so that our senses work well.

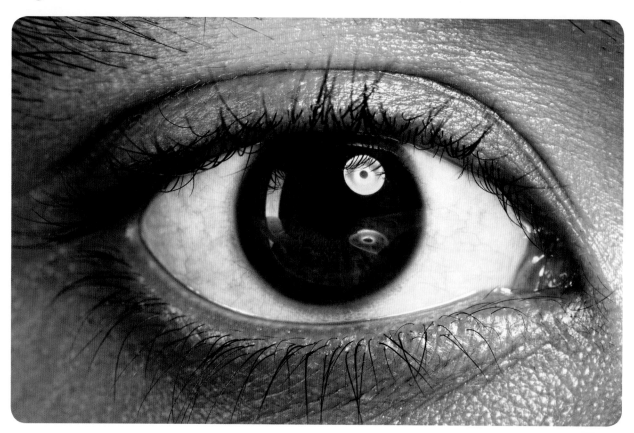

1 Look at the picture. ▲ Which sense organ does it show?

2 Which sense uses this sense organ?

3 Give some examples of things we do with our sight.

An optician is a person who can help care for our sight. They check that our eyes work well. They can tell us if we need to wear glasses.

4 Look at the pictures. ▼ What can you see?

5 Have you been to an optician? Describe what it was like.

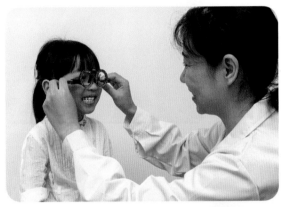

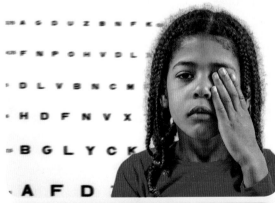

Activities

1 Look at the pictures on page 18 of your Workbook. Circle the things that we can enjoy with our sense of sight.

2 Put on a blindfold and try to do two everyday things. Do you think it will be easy to do them? Make predictions and record your findings on pages 19 and 20 of your Workbook.

3 Design a fact sheet about sight. Describe the things that our eyes help us to do and how our sight helps to keep us safe. Explain why it is important to look after our eyes.

I have learned

● It is important that we look after our sense organs.

● An optician can help to care for our eyes and our sight.

23

2.5 What do animals need to survive?

Animals, including humans need **air**, **water** and **food** to survive. Without these things, an animal will die. Animals also need to stay warm and safe.

Some animals eat only plants.
Some animals eat only meat.
Some animals eat plants and meat.

1 Look at the pictures. ▶ ▼
   Can you name the animals?

2 What are the animals eating?

3 Which of the animals can eat plants and meat?

Water comes from many different places such as rivers, lakes and wells. Fresh water is different from water in the sea. Seawater has salt in it so is not good to drink.

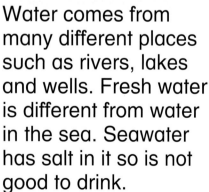

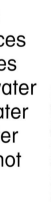

It is important that we drink clean water to stay **healthy**. Dirty water can make humans and animals ill.

4 Name two places where you can find clean drinking water.

5 Can animals drink water from the sea? Why?

Activities

1 Look at some pictures of water on page 21 of your Workbook. Tick the water that is safe to drink.

2 Think about the different types of food that your family eats. Draw and label some pictures.

3 Research a country from a different part of the world to where you live. Choose two different animals that live there. Make a poster about what the animals eat.

I have learned

- Humans and other animals need air, water and food to survive and stay healthy.
- It is important that we drink clean water.

2.6 **Humans are similar**

Key words
• human
• similar
• feature

There are lots of people in the world. We call people **humans**. All humans have some things that are the same. They have **similar features**.

1 Look at this picture of a family. ▼ What can you see?

2 How many things can you find that are the same about these people?

It is not only people in a family who have similar features. People from all over the world have some things that are the same.

3 Look at the children. ▼ What things are the same?

Activities

2 Draw pictures of your family and describe how they look similar to you.

1 Cut out some pictures of people from magazines or bring in some family photographs from home. Sort them, based on things that are the same.

3 Bring in a family photo from home. Prepare a short presentation to tell your classmates who is in the photo and describe how they are similar to you.

I have learned

- People are called humans.
- All humans have similar features.

2.7 Humans are different

Key words
• different
• unique

Humans have some features that are the same, but they also have many things that are **different**. No one is exactly the same as someone else. We are all **unique**.

Some humans are male and some are female. Some humans are tall and others are short. Humans have many different hair colours and eye colours. Some humans wear glasses and some do not. Everyone is different.

1 Look at the picture. ▶ In what ways are the children the same?

2 In what ways are the children different?

Humans are different at different ages. We grow and change as we get older. We can do different things as we get older.

3 Describe how our legs change as we get older.

4 What can you do now that you could not do when you were a baby?

Some children grow faster than other children.

5 Look at Rebecca and Kate. ▶ They are the same age. Who has grown faster?

Rebecca

Kate

Activities

1 Draw a picture of a friend. Describe what they look like. In what ways are they different from you?

2 Discuss the things that people are able to do at different ages. What can you do now that you could not do when you were 2 years old?

3 Predict who has the biggest hand span in your class. Measure your hand span on page 22 of your Workbook. Compare your hand span with your classmates' hand spans. Was your prediction correct?

I have learned

- All humans have things that are different.
- Humans are different at different ages.
- Some children grow faster than others.

Looking back **Topic 2**

In this topic you have learned

- Humans have the same body parts.
- We have five sense organs and five senses.
- Senses tell humans and other animals about their environment.
- Humans and other animals need air, water and food to survive.
- All humans have some similar features and some differences.

How well do you remember?

1 Look at the picture. ▼ What do you think the children can see? What can they hear? What can they smell? Record your answers using page 23 of your Workbook.

2 Why do humans have senses? Explain how our senses help us.

3 Think of three different animals. What food do the animals eat? What else do the animals need to survive?

Topic ③ Materials

In this topic you will learn to identify and name some common materials. You will learn how to describe the properties of different materials and how to sort objects into groups based on the properties of their materials. Lastly, you will explore how you can change materials by stretching, compressing, bending and twisting them.

Key words
- similar
- different
- feature
- sort
- group

3.1 Similar or different?

In science you often need to look at things around you and say how they are **similar** and how they are **different**. You need to be able to find **features** that are the same and features that are different.

1 Look at the picture. ▶ What can you see?

2 What things are the same?
What things are different?

You can use your observations to **sort** things into **groups**. Things that have similar features go in the same group. For example, you can make groups for size, shape and colour.

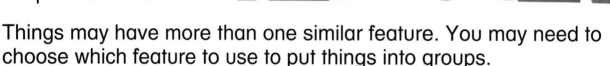

Things may have more than one similar feature. You may need to choose which feature to use to put things into groups.

3 How can you sort the bricks into groups based on features that are the same? ▼

4 What different ways can you sort the marbles into groups? ▼

You can also make groups based on features such as the type of material or the properties of a material.

5 Sort these things into three different groups. Which feature did you choose to make your groups?

Activities

1 Cut out some pictures. How are the things similar? Sort them into two groups.

2 Sort some pictures of objects on page 24 of your Workbook. Which objects can go in both groups?

3 Explore some objects and describe them. How can you sort the objects into groups?

Remember to explain how you make your groups. This will show that you understand the similarities and differences.

I have learned

- I can find features that are the same and that are different.

- I can sort things into groups with similar features.

3.2 Properties of materials

Key words
- material
- object
- properties

There are many different types of **materials**.
Materials are what **objects** are made from.
Materials have different **properties** such as their
colour, how they look and how they feel.

1 Describe the materials the objects in the pictures
are made from. ▲
What are the differences between them?

Some materials are **hard** and others are **soft**.
Some materials are **shiny** and others are **dull**.
Some materials are **smooth** and others are **rough**.

2 Look at these pictures. ▼

Which material is the hardest?

3 Why do you think this material needs to be hard?

Some materials are **heavy** and others are **light**.

Some materials are **strong** and others are **weak**.

Strong materials are difficult to break.

4 Is the bag in the picture ▲ strong? Why do you think this?

Activities

1 Make a poster to show a hard object, a soft object, a smooth object and a rough object.

2 Compare the properties of two objects. Describe how they are similar and how they are different. Record your findings on page 25 of your Workbook.

3 Look at some bags made from different materials. Predict which one is the strongest. Do an investigation to find out if you are right. Record your results on page 26 of your Workbook. Was your prediction correct? What did you do to make the investigation fair?

I have learned

- Different materials have different properties.
- Materials are what objects are made from.

3.3 More properties

Some materials are **transparent**. Things such as windows are transparent.

1 How many transparent things can you see in the picture? ▼

Some materials do not let water pass through them. They are **waterproof**. Things such as umbrellas are waterproof.

2 Name two other things that are made from waterproof material.

Key words
- transparent
- waterproof
- stretch
- elastic
- bend
- flexible
- absorbent

If a material can be **stretched** and then go back to its first shape we say the material is **elastic**. Things such as rubber bands are elastic.

Materials that can **bend** easily and do not break are **flexible**. Things such as rope are flexible.

3 What things can you use rope for?

Some materials soak up water easily. They are **absorbent**. Things such as towels are absorbent.

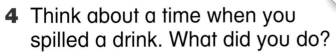

4 Think about a time when you spilled a drink. What did you do?

5 What is the difference between waterproof and absorbent?

Activities

1 Look at some pictures on page 27 of your Workbook. What are the properties of each object?

2 Choose three absorbent materials. Draw and label each one on page 28 of your Workbook. Can you name any other absorbent materials?

3 Choose three different objects to explore. How do they look and feel? What properties do they have? Draw and describe each object on page 29 of your Workbook.

I have learned

- Materials have many different properties.

3.4 What material is it?

There are many different types of **materials** in the world around us.

Wood and **stone** (rock) are found in nature. **Paper** and **cardboard** are made from wood.

A book is an **object** that ▶ is made from the material wood.

We can make **fabric** with materials such as **wool** from sheep and **cotton** from plants. ▶

cotton plants

Materials such as **metal**, **plastic** and **glass** are not found in nature. They have to be made. ▲

1 Look at the picture. ▼
   Find all the objects made from wood and plastic.

2 How many different ways has fabric been used?

3 Look at the picture. ▼
Find all the objects made
from metal and glass.

4 Can you find an object that
is made from a waterproof
material? Talk about how you
could test your object to check
it is waterproof.

5 What properties do stone and
metal have that are the same?

Activities

1 Look at some
pictures on page 30
of your Workbook.
Tick the boxes to
show which material
each object is
made from.

2 Go on a materials
hunt around your
classroom. Find
objects made from
wood, metal, fabric
and plastic. Record
your findings on page
31 of your Workbook.

3 Design a toy
made from wood,
metal and plastic.
Explain how you
used each different
material.

I have learned

● There are many different types of materials.

● Some materials are found in nature and some need to be made.

3.5 More materials

Some other common **materials** are **concrete**, **brick**, **clay**, **rubber** and **leather**.

1 Can you name some objects made from leather and rubber?

Many objects are made from several different materials.

2 What materials do you think the tablet is made from? What properties do these materials have?

3 What materials do you think the motor racing helmet is made from?

4 What useful properties do you think the food box has?

5 Name two **smooth** materials. What other properties do they have that are the same?

Activities

1 Imagine a future world with no wood. Draw what your bedroom would look like.

2 Think of three objects at home that are made from different materials. Draw and label them on page 32 of your Workbook. Describe the properties of each material.

3 Make a model bridge. Draw and label a picture to show what materials your bridge is made from. Say why you chose those materials.

I have learned

- Different materials are used to make different objects.
- The same material can be used to make different objects.
- Some objects are made from several different materials.

3.6 Sorting materials

Key words
- sort
- group
- properties

We can **sort** materials into **groups**.
We can sort by the type of material, such
as metal or wood. We can also sort by
the different **properties** of materials,
such as transparent or smooth.

1 Look at the picture. ▼
How many different materials can you find?

2 Find three objects made from glass.

3 Which objects could you sort into a group
for things made from wood?

Sometimes we can sort a material into more than one group. This is because a material can have more than one property. For example, wool is both soft and flexible.

4 Look at the pictures. ▼
Sort the objects into two groups.

5 Which properties did you use to make the groups?

Activities

1 Cut out pictures of objects made from wood, metal, plastic and fabric. Sort them into groups and stick them on pages 33–34 of your Workbook.

2 Sort some objects into groups. Can you find more than one way of sorting the objects?

3 Complete some 'odd one out' sentences on page 35 of your Workbook. Write why each one is the odd one out.

I have learned

- Materials can be sorted into groups.
- Materials in different groups have different properties.

3.7 Making smaller groups

Key words
- fabric
- plastic

There are different types of some materials. Each type can have different properties. We can sort the different types into smaller groups.

Wool, cotton, silk, polyester and nylon are all types of **fabric**. Different types of fabric are used in countries around the world for clothing.

1 Look at the pictures. ▼
Can you name the different types of fabric?

2 What do you think each fabric feels like?

There are many different types of **plastic**. Some types of plastic are very flexible and some are very hard.

44

3 Can you think of some more properties of different types of plastic?

4 Why is plastic so useful?

We can use paper in many different ways because of the properties of different types of paper. We can make things such as bags, tissues and cards all from paper.

5 Name two more things we can make from paper.

Activities

1 Talk about how we use different types of fabric to make clothes. Can you think of some other ways we use fabric?

2 Choose six different types of paper. Describe and compare the properties on page 36 of your Workbook. Write the name of each type of paper. Then stick them on page 37 of your Workbook.

3 Look at some different types of plastic. Predict which one will be the easiest to see through, the easiest to stretch and the easiest to break. Do an investigation to find out if you were correct. Draw pictures on page 38 of your Workbook to show your findings.

I have learned

- There are different types of some materials.
- Different types of a material can be sorted into smaller groups based on their properties.

3.8 Materials can change shape

Key words
- material
- squash
- bend
- twist
- stretch

We use **materials** to make things.
Look at all the objects in the pictures.

1 Say what material was used to make each thing.

You can change the shape of some materials if you **squash**, **bend**, **twist** or **stretch** them.

2 Which of the materials in the pictures can be squashed?

3 Can you bend a wooden ruler?

4 Can you twist an elastic band?

5 What could you do to change the shape of the ball of paper?

46

Activities

1 What happens if you stretch or squash an elastic band and then let go? Can you do the same thing with paper?

2 Explore some materials. Find out if you can squash, bend, twist or stretch each one. Record your findings on page 40 of your Workbook.

3 Look at some elastic bands. Which ones do you think will stretch the most? Do an investigation to find out if your predication was correct.

I have learned

- We can change the shape of some materials by squashing, bending, twisting or stretching them.

3.9 Squashing and bending

When we **squash** something, we push the material together. For example, when you squeeze a tube of toothpaste the tube is squashed and toothpaste comes out. You change the shape of the tube.

1 Look at the picture. What is ▲ the man doing?

2 What makes the clay change shape?

3 Can you squash the finished pots and change their shape? Why?

Some materials **bend** easily, such as a straw or a piece of card. We say these materials are **flexible**. Bending changes the shape of the material.

1 Make a poster to show some things in school or at home that will change shape if you squash or bend them.

2 Make a list of five materials. Write them in order from the easiest to bend to the most difficult to bend.

3 Indira has a cricket ball and a tennis ball. Predict what will happen to the shape of each ball if Indira stands on and squashes the balls. Do your own investigation to find out if your predictions were correct. Record your findings on page 42 of your Workbook.

4 Look at the pictures. ▲ Which material is the hardest to bend?

5 Why is the material hard to bend?

I have learned

- When we squash something we push the material together.
- Flexible materials can bend easily.
- We can change the shape of some materials by squashing and bending them.

49

3.10 Stretching and twisting

When we **stretch** something, we pull the material apart.

When we **twist** something, we stretch and turn the material at the same time.

If a material goes back to its first shape after it is stretched or twisted, we say the material is **elastic**.

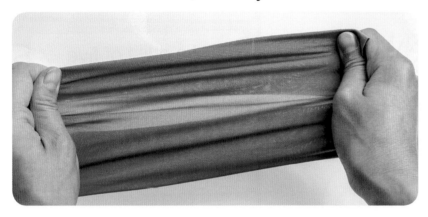

1 What happens to a balloon when you blow air into it?

2 What happens if you let the air out of a balloon?

3 Name two other things that you can stretch.

4 Do they go back to their first shape when you stop stretching them?

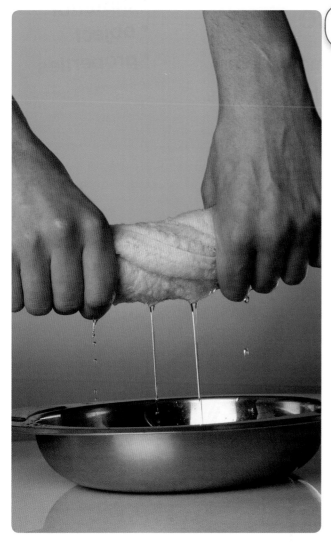

Activities

1 Make some shapes with modelling clay. Stretch and twist the clay. Draw the shapes that you make.

2 Make a pencil shape out of the clay. What is the longest shape you can make? How many times can you twist your shape before it breaks? Record your results on page 44 of your Workbook.

3 Predict what will happen if you twist a thin clay shape and a thick clay shape. Which one will break first? Do a test and record your results on page 45 of your Workbook.

5 The person in this picture is ▲ twisting the cloth to get the water out. Show how you can twist a cloth.

I have learned

- When we stretch something, we pull the material apart.
- When we twist something, we stretch and turn it.

3.11 Uses of science

Key words
- material
- object
- properties

Materials are what **objects** are made from.

1. Look at the pictures. ▼ Name the materials and the objects.

2. Describe what the objects look like.

3. What do you think the materials feel like?

Materials can be used in different ways. Different **properties** make materials better for making some things more than others.

Activities

1 Look at some pictures of things made from wood and stone. Choose one picture for each material. Stick them on page 46 of your Workbook and describe the materials.

2 Choose three different things in your classroom. Draw and describe them on page 47 of your Workbook. What is each thing used for? What properties do the materials have?

4 Look at the picture. ▲ Find the objects made from metal.

5 Why do you think they are made from metal?

3 Look at some materials. Predict which one is the most waterproof. Do an investigation to find out. Record your results. Was your prediction correct?

I have learned

- We can use different materials to make different objects.
- The properties of materials make them better for some things more than others.

Looking back Topic 3

In this topic you have learned

- There are many different types of materials.
- Different materials have different properties.
- Different materials can be used in different ways.
- Materials can be sorted into groups based on their properties.
- There are different types of some materials.
- You can change the shape of some materials by squashing, bending, stretching or twisting them.

How well do you remember?

1 Collect some different types of fabric and make a collage.

2 Look at the picture. ▼
How many different materials can you see? Can you find an object that is made from more than one material? Describe what happened when air was blown into the balloon.

3 Think about some different sports equipment. What material is each object made from? Write the properties on page 48 of your Workbook.

Topic 4 Forces and sound

In this topic you will explore, talk about and describe the movement of some familiar objects. You will learn that pushes and pulls are forces. You will explore how some objects float and some sink, and identify different sources of sounds. Lastly, you will learn that as sound travels from a source the sound becomes quieter.

4.1 Thinking and working scientifically

Key words
- investigation
- instructions
- equipment
- measurements
- observations
- record
- push

When you do an **investigation**, it is important to follow the **instructions**. Instructions tell you what you need to do and how to use the **equipment** correctly. Instructions also help to keep you safe.

1 Look at the picture. ▲ What are the children doing?

2 What instructions do you think the children have?

3 What could the instructions say to keep the children safe?

In some investigations you will need to take **measurements**. Some measurements use equipment, such as a ruler. Others may need you to count with things like hand spans.

You will often need to make **observations**. This means you have to describe what you see or what happened in an investigation.

It is important to **record** your measurements and observations. There are different ways you can do this. For example, you can write in a table or draw and label a picture.

4 Look at the picture. What are the children doing?

5 What measurements can they take?

6 What observations can they make?

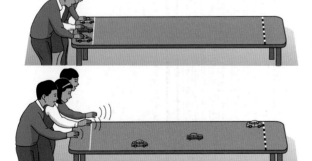

Activities

1 **Push** a ball with a small force. Then push a ball with a big force. Are they the same or different? Draw and label pictures to record your observations.

2 What do you think will happen if you give three toy cars a small push, a medium push and a big push? Predict which car will move the furthest. Plan an investigation to find out. Write instructions on page 49 of your Workbook.

3 Carry out your investigation to find out which car moves the furthest. Record and explain your investigation on page 50 of your Workbook.

I have learned

- Instructions tell us how to use equipment and how to stay safe.
- It is important to record measurements and observations.
- We can record results in different ways.

4.2 Movement

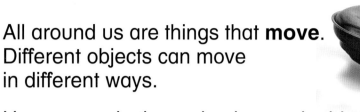

All around us are things that **move**. Different objects can move in different ways.

Humans and other animals can do things such as run, swim, jump and swing. Toys can do things such as bounce, roll and spin. Water can drip and flow. These are all different types of **movement**.

1 What can you see in the pictures? ▼

2 Can you name the different types of movement?

3 What are the children doing? ▼

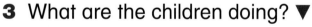

4 How many different ways can you move?

5 Look at the picture. ▶ How many different ways of moving can you find?

Activities

1 Describe how different animals move.

2 Make a poster to show how different groups of animals move.

3 Do a survey of the animals you can find near your school. Write down the different ways that the animals move on page 51 of your Workbook. What is the most common type of movement?

I have learned

- There are many different types of movement.
- Different things can move in different ways.

4.3 Pushing and pulling

Key words
- force
- push
- pull

To make an object move there needs to be a **force**. The force makes the object move.

1 Look at the pictures. ▲
What is the boy doing to make the ball move?

2 What is the boy doing to make the car move?

There are different types of forces. Pushes and pulls are forces.

▲ A **push** is a force that makes an object move away from you.

▲ A **pull** is a force that makes an object move towards you.

3 Look at the pictures. ▼
Which toys do you push?
Which toys do you pull?

4 Do any of the toys work if you push them and if you pull them?

5 Which part of your body do you use to push or pull each toy?

Activities

1 Look at some pictures on page 53 of your Workbook. Colour the pictures that show a push.

2 Choose an object that works by pushing and an object that works by pulling. Mime some actions to show how the objects work. Can your classmates guess what they are?

3 Think of some toys that you push and some toys that you pull. Draw pictures and describe how each toy works.

I have learned

- To make an object move there must be a force.
- There are different types of forces.
- Pushes and pulls are forces.

4.4 Pushes and pulls

Key words
- force
- water
- wind

We use different types of **forces** every day.
Pushes and pulls can help us to do useful jobs.

1 Look at the pictures. ▶
Which job uses a push?
Which job uses a pull?

2 Sort the pictures into pushes and pulls. ▼

Water and **wind** can sometimes push with a very big force. We can use these big forces to do useful jobs.

3 What makes the wheel in the picture turn? ▶

4 What makes the boats in the pictures move? ▼

the red boat

the blue boat

5 Which boat do you think will move faster? Why?

Activities

1 Look at the picture on page 55 of your Workbook. Circle the things that move by pushing and by pulling.

2 Make a waterwheel. What can you do to make your waterwheel move faster? Why do you think this happens?

3 Look at five different balls. Predict which balls will be the easiest and the hardest to move by blowing. Investigate to find out if you are right. Draw your predictions and your results on page 56 of your Workbook.

I have learned

- We can use forces to do useful jobs.
- Water and wind can push with a very big force.

4.5 Floating and sinking

Some objects **float** and some objects **sink**.

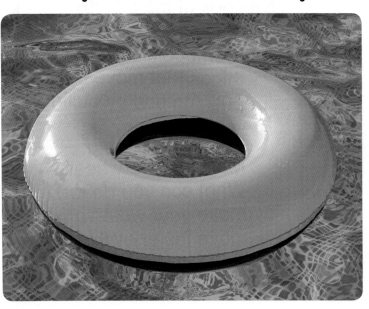

The material we use to make an object is important if we want the object to float.

1 Look at the pictures. ▼ What material is each object made from?

2 Which objects do you think will float?

3 Which objects do you think will sink?

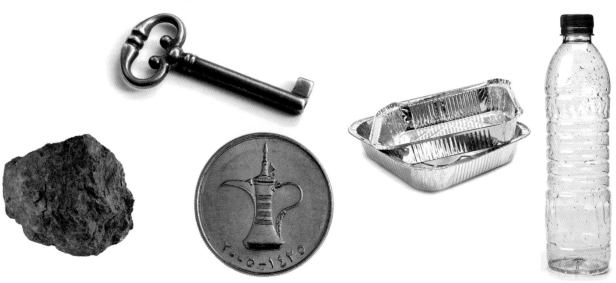

The shape of an object can also make a difference. Some objects that do not float when they are one shape, can float when they are another shape.

4 What feature of the boats helps them to float?

Activities

1 Explore some objects. Do you think they will float or sink? Write your predictions on page 57 of your Workbook. Test each object. Were your predictions correct?

2 Build the paper boats in this picture. Try floating them on water. Which shape floats the best? Explain why.

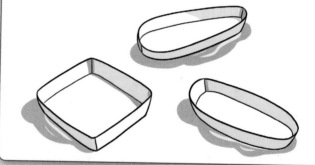

3 Choose the best boat. Put some weights on the boat to make it sink. How many weights did you use? Draw and label pictures on page 58 of your Workbook to record your findings.

I have learned

● Some objects float and some objects sink.

● The material and shape of an object can help the object to float.

4.6 Listen carefully

The world is full of different **sounds**.
Sounds are all around us.

1 Look at the picture of the children playing. ▼
What sounds would you hear if you were there?

2 Look at the picture of the busy street. ▼
What sounds would you hear if you were there?

3 Can you see anything in the pictures that does not make a sound?

Sounds come from different places.
The place or object that a sound comes from is called the **source** of the sound.

4 Look at the picture of the construction site on the next page. What sounds would you hear if you were there?

5 Can you name the source of each sound?

Activities

1 Look at some pictures of sources of sound on page 59 of your Workbook. Match them to the correct sound.

2 Be quiet and listen to your classroom. What can you hear? Make a list of the different sounds.

3 Go on a walk around your school. Write down the different sounds you can hear. Then draw and label a map of your school to show where you heard each sound, and its source.

I have learned

- Sounds are all around us.
- The source of a sound is where the sound comes from.

4.7 What made that sound?

Sounds come from many different **sources**.

Some sounds are found in nature, such as the sounds of wind and rain.

Some sounds are made by humans and other animals. We can make sounds in different ways.

1 Look at the pictures. ▼
What is the source of each sound?

2 Explain how the bell makes a sound.

3 What do you do to a whistle to make a sound?

4 What are the boys in the picture doing? ▼

5 What are the boys doing to make a sound?

Activities

1 Look at the picture on page 61 of your Workbook. Circle all the sources of sounds.

2 Listen to some sounds. Name the source of each sound. Can you name them all?

3 Look at some different musical instruments. What sound do you think each one will make? Use each instrument to make a sound. Describe how you play each one.

I have learned

- Sounds come from different sources.
- Nature, humans and other animals are all sources of sound.
- Humans can make sounds in different ways.

4.8 Loud and quiet sounds

Some sounds are **loud** and some sounds are **quiet**.

If a sound is loud, we can hear the sound from far away.
If a sound is quiet, we need to be close to the source to hear the sound. It can sometimes be difficult to hear a very quiet sound.

1 Look at the pictures. ▲ Which environment has quiet sounds?

2 Which environment has loud sounds?

3 What are the sources of the different sounds?

4 Look at the pictures. ▼▶ Sort them into loud and quiet sounds.

Some objects can make both loud and quiet sounds.

5 What do you do to make a loud sound with a drum? What do you do to make a quiet sound with a drum?

Activities

1 Look at the pictures on page 62 of your Workbook. Put the sounds in order from the quietest to the loudest.

2 Make a shaker. Draw a picture and describe the sound the shaker makes on page 63 of your Workbook.

3 Do an investigation to find out how you can change the sound that your shaker makes. What can you do to make the sound louder or quieter? Write your plan and predictions on page 64 of your Workbook. Then carry out your plan and record your results on page 65 of your Workbook. Were your predictions correct?

- Sounds can be loud or quiet.
- Some environments have loud sounds and some have quiet sounds.

4.9 Sound and distance

Key words
- distance
- source
- loud
- quiet

The **distance** between you and the **source** of a sound can affect how **loud** or **quiet** the sound is. Something loud can sound quiet if the source is far away.

As you move away from a source, the sound gets quieter and quieter until you cannot hear the sound any more.

These children are doing an investigation. They want to see how far away from a source they can walk before they cannot hear the sound anymore. When they cannot hear the sound, they will stop walking.

1 Which child do you think will stop walking first?

2 Why do you think this?

3 What other sounds can the children hear?

Activities

1 Listen to a sound. Describe how the sound changes as your teacher moves the source further away.

2 Predict what will happen to a sound when the source is in different places. Plan an investigation to find out. Write your prediction and your plan on pages 66–67 of your Workbook.

3 Carry out your investigation to find out what happens to a sound as you move further away from the source. Record your results on page 68 of your Workbook. Then compare your results to your prediction and explain your findings on page 69 of your Workbook.

I have learned

● A sound gets quieter the further away you are from the source.

73

Looking back Topic 4

In this topic you have learned

- Different objects can move in different ways.
- To make an object move there needs to be a force.
- Pushes and pulls are forces.
- Some objects float and some sink.
- Sounds are all around us.
- The source of a sound is where the sound comes from.
- Sounds can be loud or quiet.
- A sound gets quieter the further away you are from the source.

How well do you remember?

1 Look at the pictures. ▼ What forces can you see in Picture A? How many sources of sounds can you see in Picture B?

2 Make a list of different ball games on page 71 of your Workbook. Describe how you make the ball move in each game.

3 Listen and match each sound to the animal that makes the sound.

4 Think about the different sounds you can hear at home. Draw the source of each sound you can hear on page 76 of your Workbook.

Topic 5 Electricity and magnetism

In this topic you will learn about things that need electricity to work. You will also explore magnets and find out how magnets behave near different materials.

5.1 What things need electricity?

Many things we use every day need **electricity** to work. Some of these things use **mains electricity** and some use **batteries** to work.

A **device** that uses electricity has a plug. The plug goes into a socket in the wall. A device that does not have a plug uses batteries to work.

1 Look at the pictures. ▲
Which things use mains electricity?

2 Which things use batteries?

Some devices use both electricity and a battery. They use electricity to recharge the battery when it runs out.

3 Look at the picture. ▶
Find three devices
that use mains
electricity.

4 Can you find two
devices that use
batteries?

5 Which device uses
mains electricity and
a battery?

Activities

1 Look at some pictures of
devices that use mains
electricity. Match each
device to what it is used for.

2 Your teacher will give
you a picture. Colour
the things that use
mains electricity red
and the things that
use batteries blue.

3 Go on a hunt around your school. Find four things that
use mains electricity. Draw and label them on page 74
of your Workbook. Describe what each thing is used for.

I have learned

- Many things need electricity to work.
- Some devices use mains electricity and some use batteries.

5.2 Exploring magnets

Key words
- magnet
- magnetic

A **magnet** is a metal object with a special property. A magnet can pull other materials towards it. A material that moves towards a magnet is called a **magnetic** material.

Magnets can be many different shapes and sizes. You can find them in things such as toys. Magnets can also do useful jobs.

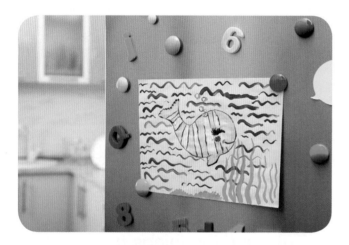

1 Look at the pictures. ▲ ▶
What can you see?

2 What useful jobs are the magnets doing?

3 Which is the biggest magnet? Why does the magnet need to be big?

4 Look at the pictures. ▶ Which things do you think are magnetic?

5 How could you test which ones are magnetic?

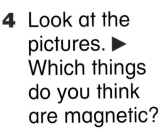

Activities

1 Look at some pictures. Tick the objects that are magnetic.

2 Use a magnet to test some objects. Are they magnetic? Record your results on page 75 of your Workbook.

3 Find four metal objects and four non-metal objects in your classroom. Test each object to find out if it is magnetic. Record your results on page 76 of your Workbook.

I have learned

- Magnetic materials will move towards a magnet.
- We can use magnets to do useful jobs.

Key words
- electricity
- device

5.3 History of science

Electricity is very important in modern life. Many things that we use every day need electricity to work.

1 Look at the pictures. ▲
Which things use electricity?

2 What do you think life would be like without electricity?

Things that we understand and know about in science change over time. In the past, people did not have electricity. Life was very different. The discovery of electricity changed many things.

3 Look at the pictures. ▲ What can you see?

4 Do you think life was harder or easier without electricity?

Devices that use electricity also change over time. Scientists are always working to find ways to make them better.

5 Look at the pictures. ▲ How have the computers changed?

Activities

1 Look at some pictures. Match the old devices to the modern devices.

2 Choose two things that were different before electricity. Draw pictures and describe them.

3 Research a device that uses electricity. Make a fact sheet to show how the device has changed over time. Has electricity made the device better?

I have learned

- What we know and understand in science is always changing.
- Life now is very different to what life was like before electricity.

Looking back Topic 5

- Many devices need electricity to work.
- Some devices use mains electricity and some use batteries to work.
- Magnetic materials will move towards a magnet.
- We can use magnets to do useful jobs.

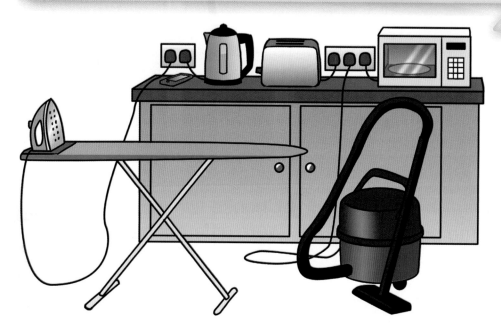

How well do you remember?

1 Look at the picture. ▲ How many things can you find that use electricity? Can you find something that uses a battery?

2 Think about things that use electricity at home. Draw and label pictures on page 77 of your Workbook. Describe what each thing does.

3 Describe what happens when you move a magnet near a magnetic material.

Topic 6 Earth and Space

In this topic you will learn that Earth is the planet that we live on. You will also learn that Earth is mostly covered in water and that land is made of rock and soil. Lastly, you will learn that the Sun is a source of heat and light, and that the Sun is one of many stars in the Universe.

6.1 Clean water investigation

Key words
* investigation
* prediction
* results

In science you can do an **investigation** to help you find the answer to a question about the world around us. Before you do an investigation, you often need to make a **prediction** about what you think will happen.

You can then do the investigation to find out if your prediction was correct. You should describe what happens and find out if your **results** are the same as your prediction.

1 Look at the pictures. ▶ ▼ Where do we get clean water from?

2 What might happen if we drink dirty water?

The children wanted to find out which source of water had the cleanest water.

3 Which water do you think is the cleanest? Which water do you think is the dirtiest?

Activities

1 Watch your teacher change some dirty water into clean water. Label the equipment on page 78 of your Workbook.

2 Predict what will happen to the dirty water when it is poured into the filter. Describe what happened. Was your prediction correct?

3 Predict which material will make the best water filter. Test the materials and record your results on page 79 of your Workbook. Did your findings match your prediction?

I have learned

- We can make predictions before we do an investigation.
- We can describe what happens during an investigation.
- We can do an investigation to find out if our prediction was correct.

6.2 Our planet Earth

Key words
- **Earth**
- **planet**
- **water**
- **land**

Earth is the **planet** that we live on. The surface of the Earth is mostly covered by **water**. The rest of the Earth's surface is **land**.

1 Look at the picture. ▼ What can you see?

2 Which parts show water? Which parts show land?

3 Why is the land different colours?

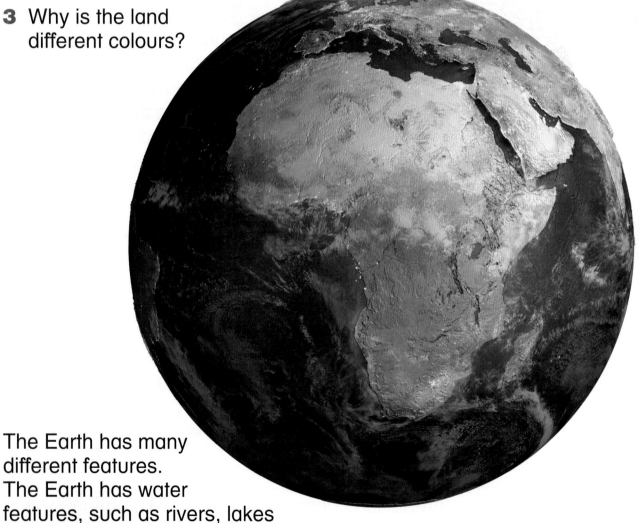

The Earth has many different features. The Earth has water features, such as rivers, lakes and seas. The Earth has land features, such as mountains, forests and deserts.

4 Look at the pictures. ▼
Can you find these features?

forest   river   lake

sea   mountain

There are different types of water on Earth. Lakes and rivers contain fresh water. Oceans and seas contain saltwater.

5 Can we drink water from the ocean? Talk about how you could find the answer to this question.

Activities

1 Make a model of the Earth. Use different colours to show the land and the water.

2 Draw and label a picture of the Earth on page 80 of your Workbook. Then complete the sentences about the Earth.

3 Choose three oceans or seas and do some research about them. Make a poster to show what you found out.

I have learned

- Earth is the planet that we live on
- Most of the Earth's surface is water.
- The rest of the Earth's surface is land.

6.3 Science and the environment

Key words
- Earth
- water
- waste
- save

Large parts of the planet **Earth** are covered in **water**. Water is very important. Animals, humans and plants all need water to survive.

1 Look at the picture. ▶ What does it show?

Some places on the Earth do not have much water.

2 Look at the pictures. ▲ Describe what you can see.

3 How are the places different?

4 What do you think it is like to live in these places?

We can use what we know about science to help the world around us. We know that water is important so we must not **waste** it. We can do things to help **save** water.

5 Look at the picture. ▲ How does it say we can save water?

6 What could this girl do to save water while brushing her teeth?

Activities

1 Play a game about how we can waste water and how we can save water.

2 Design a game. Think of the different ways that we waste water and ways that we can save water. Then play your game.

3 Design a poster to help people save water. Draw pictures and add labels to explain the ways we can save water.

I have learned

● Water is important for all living things on Earth.

● We can help the planet by saving water.

6.4 What is land made of?

The parts of the Earth's surface that are not covered by water are called **land**. Land is made of **rock** and **soil**. Rock can be broken down into smaller rocks and stones.

1 Look at the pictures. ▲ Describe the different types of land.

2 What do you think the stones and soil feel like?

Rock is a useful material that can be used to make things. Soil is important because plants grow in soil.

3 Look at the pictures. What is made ▲ ▶ from rock?

4 What properties of rock make it good for these things?

5 Look at the picture. ▼ What are the children doing?

Activities

1 Use some modelling clay and some stones to make an interesting picture.

2 Explore some rocks and stones. Draw a picture of them and include as much detail as you can.

3 Describe a stone using only your sense of touch. Then look at the stone. Was your description correct?

I have learned

- Land is the Earth's surface that is not covered by water.
- Land is made of rock and soil.

6.5 The Sun

The **Sun** is a **star**. The Sun is a **source** of **heat** and **light**. The Sun looks much bigger than other stars in the sky because it is closer to the Earth.

Key words
- Sun
- star
- source
- heat
- light

1 Look at the pictures. ▼
How are the skies different?

In the day we have light and warmth from the Sun. When the Sun goes down and disappears from the sky it becomes night. At night there is no light from the Sun, so it is dark. There is also no heat from the Sun, so it is cooler than in the day.

2 Look at the pictures. ▶
Which is night and
which is day?

3 Name some
things that you
cannot see in the
night picture.

4 Why do we
only see stars
at night?

5 Why is the Sun
important to Earth?

Activities

1 Make a model of the
Sun. Use colour to
show the heat and light.

2 Sort some pictures to show
them in order from the
brightest to the least bright.

3 Design a fact sheet about the Sun. Write and draw
pictures to describe what you know about the Sun.

I have learned

- The Sun is a star.
- The Sun is a source of heat and light.

Looking back Topic 6

In this topic you have learned

- Earth is the planet that we live on
- Most of the Earth's surface is water.
- Land is the Earth's surface that is not covered by water.
- Land is made of rock and soil.
- The Sun is a star.
- The Sun is a source of heat and light.

How well do you remember?

1 Copy the picture and add these labels.

river Sun sea rock soil

2 Name two things that we get from the Sun.

3 Think of a place that you know. Draw and label the place in the day and at night. How are they different?

4 What do you think life would be like without the Sun?

Glossary

absorbent   The property of materials such as sponges that will take in or soak up liquid easily.

air   The mixture of gases surrounding the Earth.

alive   Any living thing that is not dead.

animal   A living thing that is not a plant.

battery   Something that gives electricity to a device without a plug.

bend   To use force to make something curved or angular.

body   The whole of a person or animal, including all of their limbs and head.

danger   A situation with the possibility of suffering harm or injury.

device   A machine or tool that we use to do a job.

different   Not the same as another thing; without the same features or properties.

distance   The distance between two points is how far it is between them.

Earth   The planet that we live on.

elastic   The property of materials such as rubber that spring back when we stretch them.

electricity   Something that we use to make some devices work.

equipment   The items that you use to do a test or investigation.

fabric   Textiles or cloths.

feature	An interesting or important part or property of something.
flexible	The property of materials such as rubber that you can bend easily.
float	To rest on the surface of water.
flower	The colourful part of a plant that contains the organs from which the fruit or seeds develop.
food	Things that humans and other animals eat and need to survive.
force	A push or a pull.
group	A number of things that can be classed together, e.g. with similar features.
grow	To increase in size or amount.
healthy	In good health and feeling well.
heat	The warmth that comes from things such as the Sun.
human	A human being or person. We are humans.
instructions	A list of notes that tell you how to do something in an investigation.
investigation	An enquiry to find out something.
land	The parts of the Earth's surface that are not covered by water.
leaf	The flat green growth on the end of a twig or branch of a tree or other plant.
living	If something is living it is alive.

light	The brightness that comes from things like the Sun, stars and lamps; (when used to refer to weight) not heavy.
loud	Another word for noisy.
magnet	A special metal that pulls magnetic materials towards it.
magnetic	A material that moves towards a magnet.
mains electricity	Electricity supplied by cables and wiring through wall sockets.
material	A substance from which something is made.
measurements	Things that you can measure in an investigation.
move	To change place or position; to go in a particular direction.
movement	The action of moving.
non-living	If something is non-living it does not grow or breathe.
object	An item that is made from one or more materials.
observations	Things that you see or notice happening in an investigation.
planet	Earth is the planet on which we live.
plant	A living thing that grows in the soil and has a stem, leaves and roots.
plastic	Plastics are human-made materials, for example polythene and PVC.

prediction	A guess of what is going to happen based on knowledge of the world.
properties	The qualities or features of a particular object or thing.
pull	A force that makes an object move towards you.
push	A force that makes an object move away from you.
quiet	To make little or no sound.
record	If you record information, you write it down or put it into a computer.
results	The things that you find out in an investigation.
rock	Part of what makes up land on Earth; the other part is soil.
root	The parts of a plant that grow under the ground.
safe	Not in any danger.
senses	The physical abilities of sight, hearing, smell, touch and taste.
sense organ	The ears, eyes, nose, tongue and skin.
similar	Something that shares features or properties that are the same but not identical.
sink	To fall below the surface of the water.
smooth	A surface or texture without any bumps.
soil	Part of what makes up land on Earth; the other part is rock.

sort	To arrange or group things according to the features they have in common.
sound	Anything that can be heard. It is caused by vibrations travelling through air or water to your ear.
source	The place that something comes from.
squash	To squeeze or compress a material together.
star	A source of heat and light in the sky.
stem	The long, thin central part of a plant above the ground that carries the leaves and flowers.
stretch	To pull an object so it becomes longer than before.
Sun	One of many stars in the sky; a source of heat and light.
transparent	The property of materials such as glass that allows us to see through them.
twist	To stretch and turn something at the same time.
unique	Something that is the only one of its kind; unlike anything else.
water	The clear, colourless, tasteless and odourless liquid that is necessary for all plant and animal life; when you water a plant or an animal, you give it water to drink.
waterproof	The property of materials such as rubber that do not let water pass through them.
wind	A current of air moving across the Earth's surface.

Acknowledgements

The publishers wish to thank the following for permission to reproduce photographs.
Every effort has been made to trace copyright holders and to obtain their permission for the use of copyright materials. The publishers will gladly receive any information enabling them to rectify any error or omission at the first opportunity.

(t = top, c = centre, b = bottom, r = right, l = left)

p1 gornjak/Shutterstock, p2tl Patrick Foto/Shutterstock, p2tr ARTEM VOROPAI/Shutterstock, p2b Santhosh Varghese/Shutterstock, p5tl PeJo/Shutterstock, p5tc Eric Isselee/Shutterstock, p5tr Crisp/Shutterstock, p5tcl Butterfly Hunter/Shutterstock, p5c Gena/Shutterstock, p5bcl DenisNata/Shutterstock, p5bcr gualtiero boffi/Shutterstock, p5bl euroshot/Shutterstock, p5br Sever180/Shutterstock, p10tl & 14bl Filipe B. Varela/Shutterstock, p10br & 14br kkong / Alamy Stock Photo, p11l Maks Narodenko/Shutterstock/Shutterstock, p11cl Abramova Elena/Shutterstock, p11c oksana2010/Shutterstock, p11cr anmbph/Shutterstock, p11r Tish1/Shutterstock, p14tl Sergiu Leustean/Shutterstock, p14tr Danny Smythe/Shutterstock, p15 iofoto/Shutterstock, p22 Odua Images/Shutterstock, p23t KK Tan/Shutterstock, p23c JPC-PROD/Shutterstock, p23b atsurkan/Shutterstock, p24tr khuntong/Shutterstock, p24cl Nolte Lourens/Shutterstock, p24c Nick Fox/Shutterstock, p24cr Oksana Kuzmina/Shutterstock, p24br Landscape Nature Photo/Shutterstock, p25t & 33c Robbi/Shutterstock, p25c 3445128471/Shutterstock, p25bl W. Scott McGill/Shutterstock, p25br Angelo Ferraris/Shutterstock, p26 michaeljung/Shutterstock, p27 Rob Hainer/Shutterstock, p28t Brocreative/Shutterstock, p28bl Finomax/Shutterstock, p28bcl Gelpi/Shutterstock, p28c GOLFX/Shutterstock, p28bcr Sergey Novikov/Shutterstock, p28br Africa Studio/Shutterstock, p31 Chris Howey/Shutterstock, p32t John Kasawa/Shutterstock, p32bl 3d_kot/Shutterstock, p32br Alice Heart/Shutterstock, p33tl Richard Peterson/Shutterstock, p33tr kai keisuke/Shutterstock, p33tcl Yuriy Boyko/Shutterstock, p33tcr HomeStudio/Shutterstock, p33bcl josefauer/Shutterstock, p33bcr agoxa/Shutterstock, p33bl tose/Shutterstock, p33br Kletr/Shutterstock, p34tl Michal Dzierzynski/Shutterstock, p34tc Aleksandr Bryliaev/Shutterstock, p34tr Filip Obr/Shutterstock, p34bl magicoven/Shutterstock, p34bc RUI FERREIRA/Shutterstock, p34br Dragan Milovanovic/Shutterstock, p36 2xSamara/Shutterstock, p37t Cherkas/Shutterstock, p37tc Sagitov/Shutterstock, p37bl Crepesoles/Shutterstock, p37br Nils Z/Shutterstock, p38t Amero/Shutterstock, p38tr Jerry Horbert/Shutterstock, p38bl grynold/Shutterstock, p39tl Bedrin/Shutterstock, p39tr Andrew Buckin/Shutterstock, p39b Monkey Business Images/Shutterstock, p41t Bedrin/Shutterstock, p41b neil langan/Shutterstock, p43tl Kim Reinick/Shutterstock, p43tr photo25th/Shutterstock, p43c Elnur/Shutterstock, p43bl konzeptm/Shutterstock, p43bc photo25th/Shutterstock, p43br Ruslan Kudrin/Shutterstock, p44tl szefei/Shutterstock, p44tr Kobby Dagan/Shutterstock, p44cl andrej_sv/Shutterstock, p44cl ryby/Shutterstock, p44cr Picsfive/Shutterstock, p44bl Robbi/Shutterstock, p44br DenisNata/Shutterstock, p46tl pirtuss/Shutterstock, p46tc Mega Pixel/Shutterstock, p46tr Picsfive/Shutterstock, p46bcl Africa Studio/Shutterstock, p46bc Coprid/Shutterstock, p46br 9comeback/Shutterstock, p47t Krapivin/Shutterstock, p47tc Narongsak/Shutterstock, p47bc Nomad_Soul/Shutterstock, p47b Robyn Mackenzie/Shutterstock, p48tr wiedzma/Shutterstock, p48br Thirteen/Shutterstock, p49tl doomu/Shutterstock, p49tr Bennyartist/Shutterstock, p49bl russ witherington/Shutterstock, p49br Horatiu Bota/Shutterstock, p50 HelloRF Zcool/Shutterstock, p51 Vidux/Shutterstock, p52tl Prokrida/Shutterstock, p52tr DenisProduction.com/Shutterstock, p52bl FabrikaSimf/Shutterstock, p52bc mylisa/Shutterstock, p52br angelo gilardelli/Shutterstock, p53 Pung/Shutterstock, p55 Piti Tan/Shutterstock, p56 wavebreakmedia/Shutterstock, p58t picturepartners/Shutterstock, p58cl Kjersti Joergensen/Shutterstock, p58tc Catmando/Shutterstock, p58tr Stefanie van der Vinden/Shutterstock, p58bc lussiya/Shutterstock, p58br pirita/Shutterstock, p60l kbwills/istockphoto/Shutterstock, p60r Teri Virbickis/Shutterstock, p62tl withGod/Shutterstock, p62tr Oleksiy Mark/Shutterstock, p62br kazu/Shutterstock, p62br Ljupco Smokovski/Shutterstock, p63 Holly Kuchera/Shutterstock, p64tl Gelpi/Shutterstock, p64tr Yanik Chauvin/Shutterstock, p64c Nodmitry/Shutterstock, p64bl Stephen Rees/Shutterstock/Shutterstock, p64bcl Vladimir Sazonov/Shutterstock, p64bcr nito/Shutterstock, p64br Weera Danwilai/Shutterstock, p65 Pavel L Photo and Video/Shutterstock, p70l Steshkin Yevgeniy/Shutterstock, p70cl Serg64/Shutterstock, p70cr Eric Isselee/Shutterstock, p70r R. Gino Santa Maria/Shutterstock, p71t Vadim Ratnikov/Shutterstock, p71b Suede Chen/Shutterstock, p75 Pushish Images/Shutterstock, p76tl DD Images/Shutterstock, p76tc zirconicusso/Shutterstock, p76tr MyImages - Micha/Shutterstock, p76cl AlexLMX/Shutterstock, p76cl IvanWoW/Shutterstock, p76cr kwanisik/Shutterstock, p76br 2p2play/Shutterstock, p78tr New Africa/Shutterstock, p78cl New Africa/Shutterstock, p78cr tam_odin/Shutterstock, p78bl ESOlex/Shutterstock, p78br Petar An/Shutterstock, p79tl ajt/Shutterstock, p79tc Kapustin Igor/Shutterstock, p79cl Big Foot Productions/Shutterstock, p79c Panupong786/Shutterstock, p79bl Dan Kosmayer/Shutterstock, p79tr Picsfive/Shutterstock, p79bc SomprasongWittayanupakorn/Shutterstock, p79br outc/Shutterstock, p80tl Lee Yiu Tung/Shutterstock, p80tr JRP Studio/Shutterstock, p81l cigdem/Shutterstock, p81r CHALERMCHAI99/Shutterstock, p83 Aphelleon/Shutterstock, p84t wavebreakmedia/Shutterstock, p84c releon8211/Shutterstock, p84b A3pfamily/Shutterstock, p86 ixpert/Shutterstock, p87t Photostriker/Shutterstock, p87b Valerii_M/Shutterstock, p88t Harvepino/Shutterstock, p88cl Piyaset/Shutterstock, p88cr Atstock Productions/Shutterstock, p88bl Chatrawee Wiratgasem/Shutterstock, p88br Sawat Banyenngam/Shutterstock, p89t Supriya07/Shutterstock, p89b Monkey Business Images/Shutterstock, p90tl Luxerendering/Shutterstock, p90tcl Weepic/Shutterstock, p90tcr Stocksnapper/Shutterstock, p90tr bluedog studio/Shutterstock, p90cr amenic181/Shutterstock, p90bl Jacob L Stark/Shutterstock, p90br Weenee/Shutterstock, p92t Naeblys/Shutterstock, p92bl Roxana Bashyrova/Shutterstock, p92br Iakov Kalinin/Shutterstock.